Regla, the Quieter Side *of* Havana, Cuba

A TRAVEL PHOTO ART BOOK

LAINE CUNNINGHAM

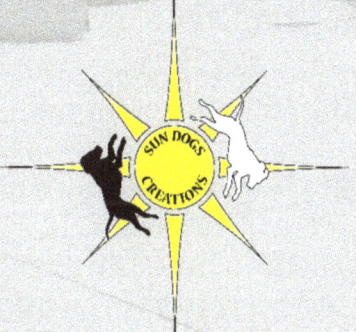

Regla, the Quieter Side of Havana, Cuba

A Travel Photo Art Book

Published by Sun Dogs Creations
Changing the World One Book at a Time
Print ISBN: 978-1-951389-18-5

Cover Image by Laine Cunningham
Cover Design by Angel Leya

Copyright © 2024 Laine Cunningham

All rights reserved. No part of this book may be reproduced in any form or by any means, electronic, mechanical, digital, photocopying or recording, except for the inclusion in a review, without permission in writing from the publisher.

Regla, one of the many municipalities that make up Havana, is accessible by a short ferry ride from the old city. Although small, the town offers visitors a lowkey day of exploring its narrow streets. Guaicanamar Park offers a place to relax after visiting the outdoor market near Plaza Guaycanamá Square and the historic Céspedes Theatre building.

One key landmark is near the dock. The old hermitage was built in 1687. The building is now a church dedicated to Our Lady of Regla where a Black Madonna is enshrined. Services blend Catholic and Santeria practices and the building, like much of the district, welcomes visitors most days.

Since Regla faces Old Havana, the views across the bay are special. The panorama includes a glimpse of the giant statue of Christ in Casablanca. Enjoy the cool breezes off the water as you consider the quieter side of Havana.

SKYBOUND

BARON

BAYSIDE

COMMUTE

CRUISE

DEMARCATION

THRESHOLD

AMUSE

HONK

SETTLEMENT

EXPEDITION

HOMELAND

CROSSOVER

TODO

ROSES

COUNTERPANE

SINEW

LAYER CAKE

SLED

PLINTH

GREIGE

AQUATIC

MUDBRICK

TABLATURE

FERMENT

SLIP

RULER

LOLLIPOP

JERKY

AUREATE

PALATIAL

HURRY

FUSE

CHILL

TITLES IN THIS SERIES

Havana, Cuba
Old Havana, Cuba
The Malecón, Havana, Cuba
Central Havana, Cuba
Vedado, Havana, Cuba
Regla, the Quieter Side of Havana, Cuba
Miramar, Havana, Cuba
Streets of Havana, Cuba
Classic Cars of Cuba
Classic Cars of Old Havana, Cuba
Classic Cars of Havana, Cuba
Spanish Colonial Havana, Cuba
Gardens of Havana, Cuba
Verge Gardens of Havana, Cuba
Cats of Havana, Cuba
Colón Cemetery, Cuba
National Art Schools of Havana, Cuba

www.ingramcontent.com/pod-product-compliance
Lightning Source LLC
Chambersburg PA
CBHW040002080526
44586CB00027B/2861